DOGS ARE GOOD PETS

By Cecilia Minden

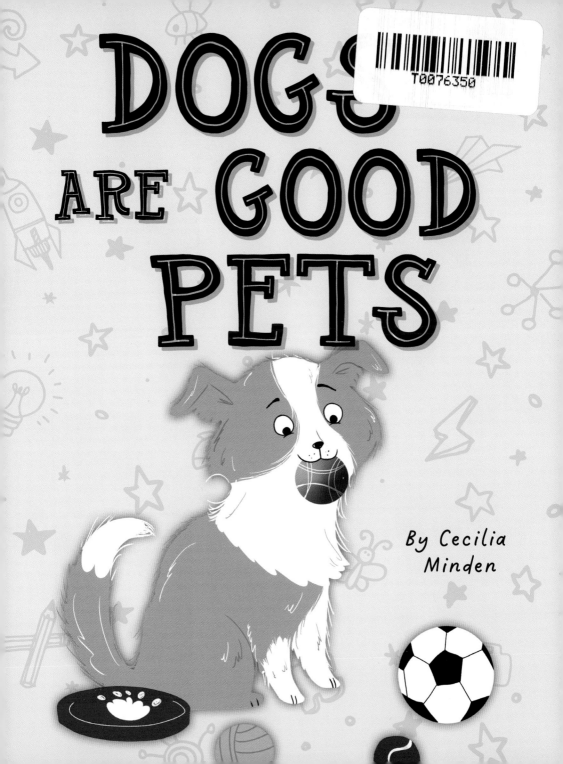

CHAPTER 1

Dogs are good pets.

Dogs can be big.

Dogs can be little.

Dogs can be a little thick.

Dogs can be a
little thin.

Dogs like to have fun.

Dogs like to have
fun with a ball.

Dogs like to have
fun with a stick.

Dogs like to have fun with a pal.

CHAPTER 2

Dogs like to run.

Dogs like to run fast.

Dogs like to run
fast with a ball.

Dogs like to run fast
with a stick.

Dogs like to jump.

Dogs like to jump on a rug.

Dogs like to nap.

Dogs like to nap on a rug.

Dogs are good pals.

Dogs are good pets.

WORD LIST

sight words

a	have	with
are	like	
be	little	
good	to	

short a words
ball
can
nap
pal
pals

short e words
pets

short i words
stick
with

short o words
Dogs
on

short u words
fun
rug
jump

107 WORDS

Dogs are good pets.
Dogs can be big.
Dogs can be little.
Dogs can be a little thick.
Dogs can be a little thin.
Dogs like to have fun.
Dogs like to have with a ball.
Dogs like to have fun with a stick.
Dogs like to have fun with a pal.

Dogs like to run.
Dogs like to run fast.
Dogs like to run fast with a ball.
Dogs like to run fast with a stick.
Dogs like to jump.
Dogs like to jump on a rug.
Dogs like to nap.
Dogs like to nap on a rug.
Dogs are good pals.
Dogs are good pets.

Published in the United States of America by Cherry Lake Publishing Group
Ann Arbor, Michigan
www.cherrylakepublishing.com

Illustrator: Sam Loman
Book Designer: Melinda Millward

Graphic Element Credits: Cover, multiple interior pages: © memej/Shutterstock, © Eka
Panova/Shutterstock, © Pand P Studio/Shutterstock, © PRebellion Works/Shutterstock

Cherry Blossom Press is an imprint of Cherry Lake Publishing Group.

Library of Congress Cataloging-in-Publication Data

Names: Minden, Cecilia, author. | Loman, Sam, 1983- illustrator.
Title: Dogs are good pets / written by, Cecilia Minden ; [illustrated by, Sam Loman].
Description: Ann Arbor, Michigan: Cherry Lake Publishing, [2023] | Series: In bloom
  | Audience: Grades 2-3. | Summary: "Are dogs good pets? Find out in this A-level
  decodable chapter book for early readers. This book uses a combination of short-
  vowel words and sight words in repetition to build recognition. Original illustrations
  help guide readers through the text"—Provided by publisher.
Identifiers: LCCN 2022042688 | ISBN 9781668918951 (paperback) | ISBN 9781668922637
  (pdf) | ISBN 9781668921302 (ebook) | ISBN 9781668926420 (hardcover)
Subjects: LCSH: Readers (Primary) | Readers—Dogs. | Dogs—Juvenile literature. |
  LCGFT: Readers (Publications)
Classification: LCC PE1119.2 .M563426 2023 | DDC 428.6/2—dc23/eng/20220919
LC record available at https://lccn.loc.gov/2022042688

Cherry Lake Publishing Group would like to acknowledge the work of the
Partnership for 21st Century Learning, a Network of Battelle for Kids.
Please visit http://www.battelleforkids.org/networks/p21 for more information.

Printed in the United States of America
Corporate Graphics